Barnyard Buddies

In the Sheep Pasture

by Patricia M. Stockland
illustrated by Todd Ouren

Special thanks to content consultant:
Roger Stockland, Farmer/Rancher
B.S. Agricultural Engineering, South Dakota State University

visit us at
www.abdopublishing.com

Printed in the United States.

Text by Patricia M. Stockland
Illustrations by Todd Ouren
Edited by Jill Sherman
Interior layout and design by Todd Ouren
Cover design by Todd Ouren

Library of Congress Cataloging-in-Publication Data
Stockland, Patricia M.
In the sheep pasture / Patricia M. Stockland ; illustrated by Todd Ouren; content consultant, Roger Stockland.
      p.cm. — (Barnyard buddies)
Includes index.
ISBN 978-1-60270-026-0
1. Sheep—Juvenile literature. I. Ouren, Todd. II. Stockland, Roger. III. Title. IV. Series.
SF375.2.S75 2008
636.3—dc22

2007004692

The sun rises. The grass is wet with dew.
The ewe stands up.

Baa, baa, baa.

The ewe's wool helps keep
her warm and dry.

The ewe has two new lambs. The lambs live with the ewe in the green pastures.

Sheep live outside in pastures.

The new lambs try to stand. Their legs are shaky. They are hungry.

Lambs can stand up by themselves only
one hour after they are born.

The hungry lambs stay near their mother. They drink milk from her. Then they shake their bellies.

Lambs shake themselves after drinking to help digest the milk. This is similar to people burping their babies.

During the spring, the lambs grow strong. Soon they get teeth. The lambs use their teeth to eat grass.

Lambs eat grass, oats, hay,
and even weeds.

During the day, the sheep graze in the pasture. Their hooves help them climb rocks and ridges.

The hard nails at the end of a sheep's
foot are called hooves. The hoof protects
the sheep from sharp edges.

The spring nights are chilly. The lambs and their mother are covered with wool. Wool keeps the sheep warm, even from rain and dew.

Wool is soft, curly hair. Farmers raise sheep for wool and meat.

The ewe and her lambs are not alone in the pasture. They are part of a flock.

A group of sheep has many names.
It can be called a flock, a herd,
or a mob.

The flock grazes together for safety.
Enemies are less likely to attack a
flock of sheep.

Animals such as coyotes and
mountain lions hunt sheep.

Sheep Diagram

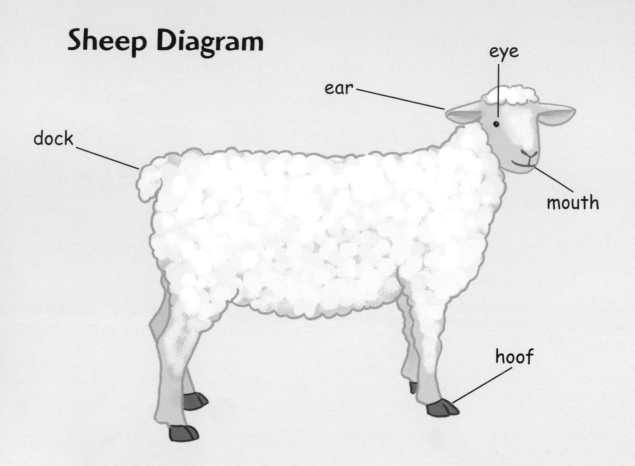

Glossary

coyote—a type of wild dog in North America.
dew—tiny drops of water.
ewe—a female sheep.
graze—to feed on land covered by grass.
mountain lion—a large, wild cat in North America.
pasture—land covered with grass that animals can eat.

Fun Facts

 The wool from a sheep can be sheared each year. This is like a haircut for the sheep. The wool is used to make fine fabrics.

 A ram is an adult male sheep. Rams are bigger and stronger than ewes and lambs.

 A good shepherd can tell the age of a sheep by looking at its teeth.

 A sheep does not have a full set of teeth on the top of its mouth. It only has top teeth in the back of its mouth.

 Lambs play by knocking their heads together. Sheep have very hard, thick skulls.

 Some sheep have horns.

 Sheep have been domesticated longer than almost any other animal.

 Sheep are raised all over the world.

Index